Our Lady Teaches About
Sacramentals
and
Blessed Objects

By
Rev. Albert Joseph Mary Shamon

Published by
THE RIEHLE FOUNDATION
P.O. Box 7
Milford, Ohio 45150

Published by The Riehle Foundation

For additional copies, write:
> The Riehle Foundation
> P.O. Box 7
> Milford, Ohio 45150

THE RIEHLE FOUNDATION
P.O. Box 7
Milford, Ohio 45150

1992

TABLE OF CONTENTS

iii

INDULGENCES

The Sacrament of Reconciliation takes away sin, but punishment due to sin remains since our sorrow for sin seldom equals the magnitude of sin (the offense against God). God forgave our first parents their sin of disobedience, but all of us still share their punishment. Punishment for sin can be removed by acts of penance, through indulgences, or through time spent in Purgatory.

An indulgence is perhaps the easiest way—Mother Church "indulging" her children, so to speak. An indulgence is the taking away of the temporal punishment due to sin already forgiven through the Sacrament of Reconciliation.

A Plenary Indulgence takes away ALL punishment due to sin. A Partial Indulgence takes away PART of the punishment due to sin.

The idea behind indulgences is to spur us on to grow in the spiritual life and to perform good works.

Prerequisites to Gain Undulgences

Partial Indulgence:
—Make the intention to gain the indulgence,
—Perform the work or prayer prescribed,
—Be in the state of grace.

Plenary Indulgence:
—Make the intention to gain the indulgence,
—Perform the work or prayer prescribed,
—Sacramental Confession must be made,
—Eucharistic Communion must be received,
—Prayer must be said for the intention of the Holy Father

A plenary indulgence can be acquired once only in the course of a day (except at the moment of death). It is further required that all attachment to sin, even venial, be absent. Although it is fitting that Communion be received and the prayer for the intention of the Holy Father be said on the same day the work or prayer is performed, the Sacrament of Reconciliation may be received eight days before or after the prescribed work or prayer.

PREFACE

This is the last booklet in my "Our Lady Says. . ." series.

The vital importance of Our Lady's appearances to us has always been in our living her messages. And her messages are never new truths, but a recall of old, forgotten truths of our Faith.

The "Our Lady Says. . ." series encapsulates the heart of Our Lady's messages given at Medjugorje.

I believe that all Medjugorje Centers in our country should devote their efforts to seeing that Mary's messages are lived. That is why I humbly suggest that all Medjugorje Centers should focus on the study, circulation and distribution of the seven booklets of the "Our Lady Says. . ." series.

Our Lady has asked for faith and conversion. Faith is believing once more in the Church's sanctifying power through her sacraments and sacramentals. Conversion is a change in lifestyle:

—by prayer and fasting (booklet 1);
—by making Holy Mass your life (booklet 2);
—by monthly confession (booklet 3);
—by knowing and living the Creed (booklet 4);
—by praying the Rosary (booklet 5);
—by loving people (booklet 6);
—by using blessed objects (booklet 7).

To show how in step Mary is with the Church, I have included in the present booklet the indulgences granted by the Church for doing the very things Our Lady has asked. These grants have been taken from the authorized English edition of the Enchiridion (Handbook) of Indulgences, issued by the Sacred Apostolic Penitentiary, 1968.

Feast of St. John Bosco
January 31, 1992

Chapter 1

WHAT ARE SACRAMENTALS?

You know, apparitions are homilies from Heaven. Apparitions never give us new truths; they only recall to our minds forgotten truths. Heresy is the revenge of a forgotten truth of the Church.

One of the forgotten truths of our age is sacramentals. For over a hundred years, Our Lady has been calling attention to sacramentals in all of her apparitions.

In November, 1831, at the Rue de Bac (Baker Street), Our Lady gave a little charity nun, Catherine Laboure, a sacramental: the Miraculous Medal.

In 1858 at Lourdes she recalled another sacramental to Bernadette: the Rosary.

In 1917 at Fatima she stressed two sacramentals: the Scapular and the Pilgrim Virgin statue which have been blessed by the popes.

In her last apparition at Fatima, October 13, 1917, she appeared robed as a Carmelite nun, holding the Rosary in one hand, and the Scapular in the other. In the twelfth century, Our Lady had said to St. Dominic that *"One day through the Scapular and the Rosary will the world be saved."* At Fatima she implied that this is the day!

On June 21, 1981, Our Lady began her apparitions at Medjugorje. In these last apparitions of hers, she has been emphasizing both the sacraments and sacramentals.

As for the sacraments, she has been urging daily Mass, if possible—*"Let Holy Mass be your life,"* and monthly confession—*"Monthly confession will be the remedy for the Church in the West."*

As for sacramentals, she keeps insisting on the use of Holy Water, holy pictures and another forgotten truth, namely, to have sacred objects blessed by priests.

Thus in 1982, Our Lady said to Mirjana:

> *"This century is under the power of the devil. . . He is destroying marriages, creating division among priests and is responsible for obsessions and murder. You must protect yourselves against these things through fasting and prayer. . .**Carry blessed objects with you. Put them in your house and restore the use of Holy Water.'** (Laurentin, The Messages and Teachings of Mary at Medjugorje, p. 301).

In 1984, Our Lady said:

"These are my last apparitions to mankind...the power of Satan which still holds, will be withdrawn from him. The present century has been under his power. Now that he is conscious of losing the battle, he is becoming more aggressive. He attacks the family... He creates divisions among the priests... **Protect yourselves, above all through prayer, through blessed sacred objects...**" (Laurentin, *idem*, pp. 309-310).

On July 18, 1985, she said to the parishioners of St. James Parish:

"Dear children! Today I invite you to **put more blessed objects in your home, and may every person carry blessed objects on himself. Let everything be blessed.** *Then, because you are armored against Satan, he will tempt you less..."* (Laurentin, *idem*, p. 267).

What, then, are sacramentals? Well, here is a short quiz. It differs from most quizzes because the answers follow:

1. What other word is "sacramental" like? (It is like "sacrament.")
2. What does the word "sacrament" mean? (It is a sign.)

3. What does the word "sacramental" mean? (It is a sign.)
4. Who gave us the sacraments? (Jesus.)
5. Who gave us the sacramentals? (The Church.)
6. What do both sacraments and sacramentals give? (They both give "grace.")
7. How do they give grace? (Sacraments give grace through the power of Jesus; sacramentals give grace through the prayers of the Church and the faith of the recipients.)

Sacramentals are sacred signs signifying spiritual effects obtained by the prayers of the Church (Canon 1166).

St. Mark tells the story of Jairus' daughter and a woman with a hemorrhage (5:21-43). Let us read it, because it will show clearly the difference between sacraments and sacramentals.

> When Jesus had crossed again [in the boat] to the other side, a large crowd gathered around him, and he stayed close to the sea. One of the synagogue officials, named Jairus, came forward. Seeing him he fell at his feet and pleaded earnestly with him, saying, "My daughter is at the point of death. Please, come lay your hands on her that she may get well and live." He went off with him, and a large crowd followed him and pressed upon him.

There was a woman afflicted with hemorrhages for twelve years. She had suffered greatly at the hands of many doctors and had spent all that she had. Yet she was not helped but only grew worse. She had heard about Jesus and came up behind him in the crowd and touched his cloak. She said, "If I but touch his clothes, I shall be cured." Immediately her flow of blood dried up. She felt in her body that she was healed of her affliction.

Jesus, aware at once that power had gone out from him, turned around in the crowd and asked, *"Who has touched my clothes?"*

But his disciples said to him, "You see how the crowd is pressing upon you, and yet you ask, 'Who touched me?'" And he looked around to see who had done it. The woman, realizing what had happened to her, approached in fear and trembling. She fell down before Jesus and told him the whole truth. He said to her, *"Daughter, your faith has saved you. Go in peace and be cured of your affliction."*

While he was still speaking, people from the synagogue official's house arrived and said, "Your daughter has died; why trouble the teacher any longer?" Disregarding the message that was reported, Jesus said to the synagogue official, *"Do not be afraid; just have faith."* He did not allow anyone to accompany him inside except Peter, James, and John, the brother of James.

When they arrived at the house of the synagogue official, he caught sight of a commotion, people weeping and wailing loudly.

So he went in and said to them, *"Why this commotion and weeping? The child is not dead but asleep."* And they ridiculed him. Then he put them all out. He took along the child's father and mother and those who were with him and entered the room where the child was. He took the child by the hand and said to her, *"Talitha koum,"* which means, *"Little girl, I say to you, arise!"*

The girl, a child of twelve, arose immediately and walked around. [At that] they were utterly astounded. He gave strict orders that no one should know this and said that she should be given something to eat.

In this story there are two miracles; both were worked in different ways. The cure of the woman with the hemorrhage happened because she took the initiative, she had faith, she touched the cloak of Jesus and her faith obtained the cure. As for the daughter of Jairus, she was dead; she could do nothing. Here, Jesus took the initiative. He asked the little girl's parents to have faith. Then, He took her by the hand and said, *"Little girl, get up,"* and at the command of Jesus, she did.

Sacramentals are the actions of the recipient. Sacraments are the actions of Christ.

Sacraments are signs instituted by Christ to give grace through His power. THEY ARE THE ACTIONS OF CHRIST. Sacramentals are signs instituted by the Church to give grace through the prayers of the Church and the faith of the recipients. THEY ARE THE ACTIONS OF THE CHURCH AND OURSELVES.

Chapter 2

WHY SACRAMENTALS?

Why does God have us use sacramentals? Mere paltry things! There are many reasons:

1. **To crush the pride of Satan.** It is beneath the dignity of God to take on Satan directly. God would not give him that satisfaction. So He used St. Michael the Archangel to kick him out of the created Heavens (*Rev.* 12:7-9), and a frail woman's seed to crush his infernal head (*Gen.* 3:15).

Oliver Wendell Holmes, in his *Autocrat of the Breakfast Table,* asks this question: "If a fellow attacked my opinions in print, would I reply? Not I." And the reason he gave for not responding was the Hydrostatic Paradox of Controversy. Then he explained: "Take a bent tube, one arm of which was the size of a pipe-stem, and the other big enough to hold the ocean. Water would stand at the same height in one as in the other. *Controversy equalizes wise men and fools in the same way*—and the fools know it" (p. 89).

8

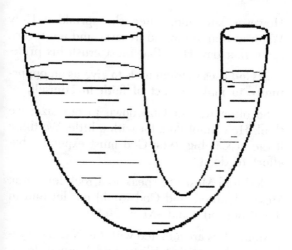

For God the Creator to take Satan on directly would dignify the fiend. Instead, God uses creatures, the weak things of the world, to confound the proud. Imagine mighty Lucifer being curbed by such weak and simple things as water, the Sign of the Cross, beads, a cloth Scapular.

Our Lady said this to Fr. Gobbi, *"The red dragon will find himself decisively humiliated and defeated when I bind him, not by a great chain, but by a very frail cord: the holy Rosary"* (To The Priests, Our Lady's Beloved Sons, #275).

St. Teresa of Avila tells us in her autobiography that when the devil attacked her in bodily form and she made the Sign of the Cross, he would fly away but return again later that day.

However, she said, when she sprinkled Holy Water at him, he would fly away and not return again that day. How that must crush his pride.

2. **God uses sacramentals to give us an opportunity to make an act of faith in Himself.**

So often we cut God down to our size; we think He cannot do a lot with a little. We think if the task is big, then God must expend a big effort to do it.

God told Moses to speak to a rock for water. Moses doubted, and God would not let him in the Promised Land (*Num.* 20:6f).

Many of us are afflicted with the Naaman syndrome. The prophet Elisha told Naaman to go bathe seven times in the Jordan, and his leprosy would be cured. Naaman was furious; there seemed to be no proportion between the problem and the cure. Naaman would have shunned the cure had it not been for the better judgment of his servants (*2 Kings* 5). God can do a lot with a little.

God demonstrated the same thing to the Apostles. When there was a problem of feeding 15,000 people, they never believed five loaves could solve it (*Jn.* 6:1f). They didn't take God into consideration. God can do a lot with a little. That's what sacramentals say. We must believe.

3. **God uses sacramentals to accommodate Himself to our limitations.** We are not angels—

pure spirits who can communicate by extra-sensory perception (ESP). We are animated bodies. All our knowledge comes to us through our five senses. *Nisi in intellectu nisi quod prius est in sensu*—which means, "There is nothing in our minds that has not first come through our senses." Thus, a person born blind cannot conceive of color.

> My senses five are five great Cups
>   Wherefrom I drink delight!
> For them to God a grace I sing
>   At morning and at night,
> For five fair loving cups are thy
>   That feed me with delight.
>
>   (Rachel Taylor)

That is why the Church has her rites and rituals in her liturgy and worship of God.

When Jesus cured the blind man, He smeared mud on his eyes and told him to go wash in the pool of Siloam (*Jn.* 9:1-7).

On the deaf-mute, Jesus used spittle, touched his mouth and ears and said, "Ephphatha" (*Mark* 7:34).

4. Finally, **sacramentals are an attempt to bring our daily lives into a continuing relationship with God.**

It is strange, is it not, that so often the sophisticate who pooh-poohs holy pictures, medals or Rosaries, himself uses mementos and keepsakes

11

when he is in love. Photos, pins, rings—aren't these just some of the trappings lovers use?

So God who loves us would have us who love Him use mementos, keepsakes.

Statues and images have SUGGESTIVE POWER. They remind us of God and the saints of God. What books are to those who read, statues and images are to those who do not or cannot read. One picture is worth 10,000 words. Arnold Lunn called the stained glass windows of the great cathedrals of Europe "the bibles of the poor."

If you travel in France and Spain and visit the great cathedrals there, you will be horrified, as I was, by the mutilations of the statues of the saints. You can still see the scars inflicted by the French revolutionaries on the exquisite statues of Notre Dame of Paris. The revolutionaries were wise: to get rid of God, get rid of the reminders of God. Out of sight, out of mind.

Iconoclasm, or statue-smashing, was condemned as early as the eighth century by the Second Council of Nicea (787). Thus, the Council defined: "We admit that images should be venerated. Those of us who are not so minded we subject to anathema..." (DB #306).

The Council's reasons for condemning iconoclasm was precisely for this same reason, namely, that statues and images have suggestive power.

The Council further said that "the honor of the image passes to the original." From the image we learn what we must adore; we do not adore the image.

Sin is a turning from God to creatures; sacramentals reverse the process and turn us from creatures to God. Sacramentals help us not to forget God.

When a Marian Cenacle of priests had recited the Rosary around her statue, Our Lady said to Fr. Stefano Gobbi (1/24/84):

"Beloved Children, I welcome this Rosary you are reciting together with such great love and fervor.

"As a mother I want to tell you that I am here with you, represented by the statue you have here. Each of my statues is a sign of a presence of mine and reminds you of your Heavenly Mother. Therefore, it must be honored and put in places of greater veneration.

"Just as you look with love at a photograph of a cherished person because it transmits to you a reminder and a likeness, so too you should look with love at every image of your Heavenly Mother, because it transmits to you a reminder of her, and still more, it becomes a particular sign of her presence among you.

13

"How deeply saddened I am by the fact that I am, so frequently today, ousted from the churches. Sometimes I am placed outside, in a corridor, like some trinket; sometimes I am put in the back of the church, so that none of my children can venerate me." (#283).

There are two extremes to avoid regarding sacramentals:

One is SUPERSTITION—to treat the sacramentals as if they have magical powers. Superstition exists when we try to get an effect without a proportionate cause, for instance, to think a rabbit's foot can bring good luck. In the sacramentals there is a proportionate cause to the effects desired; the power of the sacramentals comes from the prayers of the Church and the faith of the recipient. Blessing one's throat on St. Blaze's day is no infallible guarantee against a sore throat. Sometimes an illness can be more beneficial to a person than a cure. However, the blessing will help, as God sees fit. The sacramentals are not magical charms; they are a calling upon God to act.

The other extreme is SOPHISTICATION—to pooh-pooh the sacramentals as the tools of the weak and ignorant. The trouble with the sophisticated person is that he or she seeks to shape God according to their own image and likeness, to cut Him down to their size. They seek God their way, not His way. Thus, Lucifer rebelled against God, for he never thought God would become a man; and the Jews rejected the Messiah, because they never thought the Messiah would be a suffering Servant. *"My ways are not yours."*

*   *   *

What does the Church think about sacramentals?

In her Enchiridion of Indulgences, she writes: "The faithful who devoutly use an *article of devotion* (crucifix or cross, Rosary, Scapular or medal) properly blessed by any priest, obtain a *partial indulgence*" (#35).

(In order to bless an article of devotion properly, the priest uses the prescribed formula; otherwise, he makes a simple Sign of the Cross toward the article of devotion, audibly adding the words, "In the name of the Father, and of the Son, and of the Holy Spirit.")

Chapter 3

THE SIGN OF THE CROSS

We make a cross by tracing our right hand from forehead to breast, from left to right shoulder. This Sign of the Cross expresses our belief in the mystery of our redemption.

To the cross-sign, we add the words, "In the name of the Father, and of the Son, and of the Holy Spirit," to express our belief in the Holy Trinity, another great mystery of our salvation. The Trinity tells us that, even though God is one, He is not an alone God, because He is a Community of three loving Persons.

We express the oneness of God when we use the words "in the name of," for we use the singular "name" and not the plural "names."

And we express who the three Persons are in the one God by the words, "the Father, the Son, and the Holy Spirit." Because these three Persons are equal, we join Them together by the coordinate conjunction "and." We say, "and of the Father," "and of the Son," "and of the Holy Spirit." Those "and ofs" are very important for they express the equality of the three Persons.

When we say, "In the name of the Father," we touch our forehead, for the Father is the head of the Trinity. When we say, "and of the Son," we touch our breast, for the Son came to teach us of the love of the Father for us, and love is in the heart. When we say, "and of the Holy Spirit," we touch first our left shoulder at the word "Holy" and then our right shoulder at the word "Spirit," for the Holy Spirit is the strength of God, the Comforter, who helps us carry the burdens of life. We carry heavy things on our shoulders.

We go from the left shoulder to the right for two reasons: first, we write from left to right (in the East, they write from right to left; therefore they sign themselves that way—from right shoulder to left); and secondly, sin puts us on the left hand of God, but the forgiveness of sin brings us to the right side of God, and sins are forgiven by the Holy Spirit. "Receive the Holy Spirit," Jesus said when instituting the sacrament of Penance. "Whose sins you forgive are forgiven them" (*Jn.* 20:22-23).

In history, God demonstrated the power of the cross by using it to bring the pagan Roman Empire to an end. After the death of Diocletian, Constantine the Great inherited the poorest portion of the Roman Empire—Briton and Gaul.

All of Italy was given to the pagan Maxentius. Militarily, Maxentius had more than double the power and strength of Constantine's army. So Constantine's officers were overwhelmingly against his invading Italy.

But in the springtime of 312 A.D., Constantine, on the march with his army in Gaul, saw a cross in the sky in front of the sun with the words *In hoc signo vinces* ("In this sign you shall conquer"). Constantine ordered the cross to be put atop his battle standards. After this vision, all his doubts about invading Italy vanished and gave way to absolute certainty. Fearlessly and with lightning rapidity, he descended into Italy and engaged Maxentius in battle. Although outnumbered four to one, Constantine won a decisive victory. Maxentius and his troops retreated to Rome. The only bridge for them to cross the Tiber was the Milvian Bridge. But under the weight of the numbers of fugitives, the bridge collapsed, and Maxentius fell into the Tiber, and in his heavy armor, drowned.

The next day, October 29, 312, Rome opened its gates to Constantine, who entered it in triumph. Constantine always attributed his victory to the cross. In thanksgiving, he ended the persecution of the Church, gave her legal status, and outlawed death by crucifixion. Later on, his mother, St. Helena, went to Jerusalem and found the relic of the true cross of Christ.

St. John Vianney, the Cure of Ars, used to say that the Sign of the Cross is formidable, because by it we escape the power of the devil. Even in the movies, Dracula is depicted as shrinking away from the cross.

Often Jesus taught, *"Whatever you ask in my name, I will do"* (*Jn.* 14:13). Imagine the blessings that flow to us when we begin what we do "in the name" of the Most Holy Trinity! No wonder we say, when we make the Sign of the Cross, that we are blessing ourselves!

Lastly, by the Sign of the Cross, we sign over to God, so to speak, all that we do. When Columbus took America *in the name of* Isabel and Ferdinand of Spain, it became a Spanish possession. Similarly, whenever we do anything in the name of the Trinity, we sign it over to Them, thereby sanctifying our actions and making them redemptive.

Parents should sign their children with the cross when they kiss them goodnight before going to bed.

*　　*　　*

What does the Church think about the Sign of the Cross?

In her Enchiridion of Indulgences, she writes, "A *partial indulgence* is granted to the faithful, who devoutly sign themselves with the Sign of the Cross, while saying the customary words: *In the name of the Father, and of the Son, and of the Holy Spirit. Amen."* (#55).

Prayer Before a Crucifix

Look down upon me good and gentle Jesus, while before Thy face I humbly kneel and with burning soul pray and beseech Thee to fix deep in my heart lively sentiments of faith, hope and charity, true contrition for my sins and a firm purpose of amendment, while I contemplate with great love and tender pity Thy Five Wounds, pondering over them within me and calling to mind the words which David thy prophet said of Thee my Jesus, "They have pierced My Hands and My Feet, they have numbered all My Bones." *(Ps. 21:17-18)*

Our Father, Hail Mary, Glory Be, for Holy Father's intentions;

Plenary indulgence when said after Communion; (S. Paen. Ap., 2 Feb. 1934)

Chapter 4

HOLY WATER

Water is a sign of cleansing. God Himself prescribed its use for His people as a rite of purification (*Numbers* 19).

The Jews purified themselves with water before entering the Temple. The Church imitated this ceremony by placing water at church doors so that the faithful could wash their hands and faces for Mass.

As early as the fourth century, this water was blessed, and the custom arose of using "Holy Water" on other occasions.

In the ninth century, Pope Leo IV prescribed that in parish churches on Sunday, water should be blessed to be sprinkled on the people and used in their homes.

The Holy Water derives its power from the prayers of the Church. The Church is the Bride of Christ, and He always hears the prayers of His Spouse.

Parents should sprinkle each bedroom with Holy Water before going to bed, for the devil cannot long abide in a place or near persons often sprinkled with Holy Water.

Whenever I sprinkle Holy Water, I always throw some for the relief of the souls in Purgatory. I believe it helps them greatly.

The Mother of God knows the power of Holy Water. That is why she has been urging its use in her messages at Medjugorje. In 1982, to Mirjana, she said, *"Carry blessed objects with you. Put them in your house, and restore the use of Holy Water"* (Laurentin, *"Messages and Teachings"* p. 301).

* * *

To grasp some idea of the power of Holy Water, one ought to ponder on the prayer-formula of the Church, used by the priest, in blessing Holy Water. The prayer-formula is a bit lengthy, but I prefer it to merely making the Sign of the Cross over water. The Sign of the Cross gives us blessed water, but the prayer-formula gives us Holy Water.

* * *

The formula for blessing Holy Water can be found in the Appendix.

Chapter 5

THE SCAPULAR

1. What is the Scapular?

A Scapular is two pieces of brown, rectangular cloth, attached by two strings. It is worn over the shoulders so that one piece of cloth lies on one's breast and the other on one's back. The name "Scapular" comes from the fact that it is thrown over the shoulders, and the Latin word for "shoulder" is *scapula*.

The Scapular as we know it today is an abbreviation of the Scapular worn by the religious of Mt. Carmel, the Carmelites. Like so many monks, the Carmelites' motto was *Ora et Labora*—Pray and Work.

They generally worked as farmers. That posed a problem. Their robes were cream-colored. How could they keep them clean, working in the fields? When mothers work in the kitchen, they generally put on an apron to prevent soiling their dress. So the monks devised an apron for working in the fields.

Their apron was a long rectangular piece of brown cloth with a hole in the center. The monks simply tossed this "apron" over their heads and upon their shoulders when going out to work. It covered them, front and back, from the shoulders almost to the ground, like a sandwich board worn by picketers. Thus, they kept their robes clean.

Since it was inconvenient for lay persons in the world to wear this lengthy Scapular, it was considerably reduced to its present size.

2. How did we get the Scapular?

The Carmelite Order was founded about 1154 A.D. on Mt. Carmel, overlooking Haifa and the Mediterranean Sea. When the Saracens defeated the Crusaders in the twelfth century, the Carmelites were driven out of Mt. Carmel. They returned to Europe, but like most transplants, the Order began to languish and wither.

In England at the time, there lived a young lad who had shown extraordinary piety since his youth. At the age of 12, he had retired to the woods in southwestern England and for over twenty years had dwelt in the hollow of an oak tree. That was how he got his name St. Simon Stock (1165-1265). He often conversed with Our Lord and Our Lady. During one of these Heavenly meetings, the Blessed Virgin Mary revealed to Simon to seek the company of those hermits known as the Carmelites, who had recently come to England.

Abandoning his forest home, he entered the Order at Aylesford, near Rochester in Kent. He could not hide his holiness, and so, within two years, he was chosen to head the Order in 1245. He was 80 at the time, and the Order was in deep trouble. So, in 1251, Simon went to a monastery in Cambridge and prayed earnestly to the Mother of God for the Order.

On July 16, 1251, while in ecstasy, the Mother of God appeared to him, surrounded by angels. She held in her hands the full Scapular of the Carmelite habit and, with utmost compassion, said to Simon:

> *"Receive, my beloved son, this Scapular of thy Order. It shall be the mark of the privilege I have obtained for you and all the Carmelites; whoever dies clothed with this holy Scapular shall not suffer eternal fire."*

There soon came a complete transformation within the Carmelite Order. The privilege of wearing the Scapular was extended to those who became members of the Confraternity of Our Lady of Mount Carmel, and for them it was abbreviated to the form now worn by the laity enrolled in the Confraternity.

3. **Whence the power of the Scapular?** There are four reasons why the Scapular is so powerful.

a. **The first reason is, because of the Promise of the Mother of God.**

Mary, the Mother of God, promised St. Simon Stock that who wore this Scapular would be saved from eternal fire, and Mary keeps her promises. She *can* keep them, because she is the Mother of God, and God, who commanded us to honor our father and our mother, will never deny His own Mother, Mary, any request she makes. That is why St. Alphonsus Ligouri called Mary "almighty." He, Who is almighty by nature, makes her almighty by her intercession, for He refuses her nothing!

Generally, when I speak about the Scapular to grade school kids, I bring in a newspaper that has a yellow and red page filled with coupons. The supermarkets call this a Coupon Blitz. Each coupon promises to give you some product, but at reduced price with the coupon. For example, with a coupon, you can get waffles at two for one dollar, or a four-pack of bath tissue for 48 cents, or two dozen eggs for the price of one, with a coupon, and so on.

Then I would ask the kids, "Do you really believe this? Do you think that this coupon, this yellow piece of paper, can save you all this money?"

"Of course," they would all answer.

"But it's only a piece of paper," I would say. "How come?"

"Well, the supermarket pledges to honor these. It says so on the coupon."

"You really believe that?" I would ask with an incredulous look.

And again they would say, "Yes," and look at me as though I were stupid.

Ah, then I would hold up a Scapular, and I would read what is written on one of the pieces of cloth, namely, "Whosoever dies wearing this Scapular shall not suffer eternal fire."

"This," I would say, "is the Mother of God's coupon. She says, 'Wear this and you won't go to Hell.' Do you believe her?"

If they answered, "Yes," I would say, "The proof of the pudding is in the eating—are you wearing a Scapular now?"

If they were not, I would say, "See, you believe a supermarket ad, but you don't believe the Mother of God. You believe a coupon can save you money, but you don't believe Mary's coupon can save you from Hell."

Then I would generally enroll the class in the Scapular.

b. The second reason why the Scapular is so powerful is because of the prayers of the Church.

The Church is the Spouse of Christ, and Christ always hears the prayers of His Bride. Here are the words the Church uses in blessing a Scapular:

O Lord Jesus Christ, Savior of mankind, by Thy right hand sanctify these Scapulars (this Scapular) which Thy servants will devoutly wear for the love of Thee and of Thy Mother, the Blessed Virgin Mary of Mt. Carmel, so that, by her intercession, they may be protected from the wickedness of the enemy and persevere in Thy grace until death, Who livest and reignest for ever and ever.

THE PRIEST THEN SPRINKLES THE SCAPULAR WITH HOLY WATER, AFTER WHICH HE PLACES THE SCAPULAR ON EACH ONE, SAYING:

Receive this blessed Scapular and ask the Most Holy Virgin that, by her merits, it may be worn with no stain of sin and may protect you from all harm and bring you into everlasting life. Amen.

The Church asks Jesus to give to the devout wearer of the Scapular two tremendous graces: protection against the evil one and perseverance in the grace of God until death.

What the Church asks for on earth, God gives in Heaven.

c. The third reason why the Scapular is so powerful is that it enrolls one in the Carmelite Order.

When one is enrolled in the Scapular, one is incorporated into the Carmelite Order. After putting the Scapular around the candidate's neck, the priest goes on to pray:

By the power granted me, I admit you to share in all the spiritual works performed, with the merciful help of Jesus Christ, by the Religious of Mount Carmel, in the name of the Father, and of the Son, and of the Holy Spirit. Amen.

Imagine that! We share in the good works of Sr. Lucia (the last surviving seer of Fatima, now a Carmelite) and all the prayers and works of the other Carmelite priests and sisters. No wonder Mary can promise Heaven to those consecrated to her by wearing the Scapular.

d. Lastly, the Scapular is so powerful, because of the faith of the wearer.

When we pledge to wear the Scapular, we also pledge to live in the spirit of the Carmelite Order. Every religious order has three vows: poverty, chastity and obedience.

When we put on the Scapular, we pledge to live the spirit of poverty: to become detached from material things—to use them, but not make a god of them.

Henry VIII offered St. Thomas More all that this world could give in riches and honors, if only the holy man would endorse the king's divorce so he could remarry. St. Thomas refused, saying, "I am the king's good servant, but God's first." That's the spirit of poverty—a willingness to give up the whole world rather than lose one's soul.

Wearing the Scapular is also a pledge to observe the spirit of obedience: *sentire cum ecclesia*—to think with the Church: to embrace her values, ideals and truths. To assent, not dissent, with the Church, even when she condemns artificial contraception.

Finally, to put on the Scapular is to pledge to live the spirit of chastity according to one's state in life—to imitate Mary, especially regarding modesty. Just note the modesty in dress of Mary in all of her apparitions. She is clothed from neck to feet.

So the wearing of the Scapular is no rabbit's foot, no magical charm. It has power because of Mary's promise, the Church's prayers, the prayers and good works of the Carmelite Order and your own endeavor to live the spirit of the three vows.

To Mariamante, Our Lady said:

"The Scapular of Mount Carmel is a sign of my protection. Wear it always. It will help you to do good because it is a sign of my love and will remind you of me often. This is the purpose of all sacramentals— to remind you of the person behind them and to help you to imitate their virtues. The Scapular and the Rosary are the greatest of these and will afford you the most protection. I want all my children to wear one. It will help them to love Jesus more. This is a simple means by which God helps His children. Wear it always." (*The Apostolate of Holy Motherhood*, pp. 10-11.)

4. **The Scapular that saved two lives in World War II.**

This is a true story. Here is how the one told it to whom it happened.

I was a member of the Irene Brigade. One evening we encamped at an old farm near Nijmegen. Behind the house was the old wooden pump. It was a great opportunity to wash away the sweat and dust of hours of fighting, so I tossed my jacket to the ground and hung up my Scapular on the pump while I washed. An hour later, we received orders to proceed about a mile and half farther to occupy a trench there.

We all looked forward to getting a good night's sleep in that trench.

When I was about to lie down and was unbuttoning my collar, I realized to my horror that I no longer had my Scapular. It had been a gift from my mother. I had it with me all during the war. To go fetch it was unthinkable, so I tried to go to sleep. I couldn't. All around me my buddies were sleeping like logs. Finally, overcome by the desire to get the Scapular back, I crept out among my sleeping companions. It was pitch dark, but in a short time I was back on the farm. I searched all over the pump for my Scapular, but it was gone.

I was about to strike a match when there was a dreadful explosion. Was this an enemy attack? I raced back to our trench. Near the trench, I saw engineers clearing away piles of dirt and barbed wire. At the very spot where my companions had been sleeping, there yawned a gigantic shell-hole. Before they had vacated this trench, the enemy had placed a time-bomb in it, and it had exploded during my absence. Nobody survived the explosion. If I had not set out to fetch my Scapular, I would have been buried under that rubble too.

The next morning at the field kitchen, I met a buddy there. He looked at me with astonishment. "I thought you were in that trench!

"And I thought **you** were buried there," I said.

My friend continued, "I was lying in that trench, but before I went to sleep, I went looking for you. I couldn't find you. The corporal saw me hunting around and asked me what I wanted. When I told him, he said, 'Be sensible! Go to that inn nearby, and get me a bottle of water.' While I was on this errand, the explosion occurred."

"Well, I escaped it by a hair's breadth too," I replied. "But why on earth were you looking for me so late at night?"

"To give you this," he answered, and he handed me my Scapular which he had taken from the old pump.

5. The Scapular medal.

Early in this century, missionaries petitioned Rome to allow a medal to be used, instead of the cloth Scapular, in the tropics, for in the excessive humidity in the tropics, it was hard to keep the cloth Scapular from deteriorating.

On December 16, 1910, Pope St. Pius X granted permission for the use of a Scapular medal, with the image of the Sacred Heart on one side and an image of Our Lady on the other.

It would possess the same promises and indulgences as the brown Scapular. However, the Holy Father said, "I desire most vehemently that the cloth Scapulars be worn as heretofore."

Incidentally, I wear both the medal and the cloth Scapular. Only when I shower or go swimming do I take off the cloth Scapular. I think this is the spirit of the pope's directive.

Our Blessed Mother updated the Scapular Devotion at Fatima in her last apparition there October 13, 1917. In her last apperance, she held her Divine Son in her left arm, was dressed in the Carmelite Habit, and in her right hand she held out the Scapular. Sister Lucy, who saw her, stated that Our Lady wishes all to wear the Scapular as the sign of consecration to her Immaculate Heart.

The Scapular is the livery of Mary and the garment of her grace and protection. Wear it with love and devotion.

Each morning, kiss the Scapular after you make the Morning Offering. Touch it in times of temptation; that is like clasping her hand. Say the prayers, "Sacred Hearts of Jesus and Mary, protect us!"

* * *

The Sabbatine Privilege. This Privilege is that Mary promises to release from Purgatory on the first Saturday (hence the name "Sabbatine") after death all those who: (1) wear the brown Scapular; (2) observe chastity according to their state in life; and (3) say the Little Office of the Blessed Virgin Mary every day. For those who find it impossible to say the Little Office each day, a priest with proper faculties could grant the substitution of abstinence from meat on Wednesdays and Saturdays or the five decades of the Rosary.

*   *   *

The formula for the Enrollment in the Scapular is in the Appendix.

Chapter 6

MEDALS

Medals are conferred on soldiers. They call to mind acts of heroism and bravery. So Mary gave to St. Catherine Laboure a medal to remind us of her Immaculate Conception and of her power to obtain graces for her children.

Catherine Laboure was born in a little Burgundian village, Fainles-Moutiers, on May 2, 1806. She was the ninth child in a family of eleven. God, who had marked Catherine out for holiness, permitted her to suffer from a very early age. She was only nine when she lost her mother, Louise. Deprived of a mother's love, Catherine, at age nine, took Mary as her mother.

In answer to God's call, Catherine, at the beginning of the year 1830, entered the Daughters of Charity of St. Vincent de Paul. During her first months in the novitiate at the Motherhouse at 140 Rue du Bac in Parish, Catherine was favored by many apparitions of Our Lady.

On a Saturday before the First Sunday of Advent, November 27, 1830, Catherine was in the chapel at 5:30 for evening prayers. Here is what happened then:

"Suddenly I heard a sound like the rustle of a silk dress. When I looked in that direction, I saw the Blessed Virgin. She was standing, dressed in a robe of white silk, like the dawn, her feet resting on a globe, only half of which I could see. In her hands, at the level of her breast, she held a smaller globe, her eyes were raised toward Heaven...her face was indescribably beautiful...

"Then suddenly, I saw rings on her fingers, covered with jewels, some large and some small, from which came beautiful rays... At this moment...an interior voice spoke to me:

" *This globe which you see represents the entire world, particularly France...and each person in particular.'*

" [The rays are] *a symbol of the graces which I shed on those who ask me.'*

"Then an oval shape formed around the Blessed Virgin, and on it were written these words in letters of gold: 'O Mary conceived without sin, pray for us who have recourse to thee.'

"Then I heard a voice say:

'Have a medal struck after this model. Those who wear it will receive great graces; abundant graces will be given to those who have confidence.'

"Some of the precious stones gave forth no ray of light. *'Those jewels which are in shadow represent the graces for which people forget to ask me.'*

"Suddenly the oval seemed to turn. I saw the reverse of the medal: the letter M surmounted by a cross, and below it, two hearts, one crowned with thorns, and the other pierced by a sword. Enclosing the entire picture were twelve stars within a golden frame.

"I seemed to hear a voice which said to me: *'The M and the two hearts say enough.'* Mary, Jesus. . .the sufferings of both united for our redemption."

The message of the medal is clear. The globe on which Mary stood represents the sins of the world, for the serpent on the globe is the symbol of sin. Mary's heel is on the serpent's head, for she is the woman who will crush him.

To save man from sin, God sent His Son, Jesus, born of the Virgin Mary, who was "conceived without sin."

Jesus came to our world and expressed a love without limit by giving His life on the cross in conjunction with Mary—symbolized by the cross and the two hearts.

As from the side of the sleeping Adam came Eve, so from the side of the dying Christ came His Bride, the Church, founded on the twelve apostles—symbolized by the twelve stars.

In May 1832, the medal was struck and distributed throughout France. It was called the Medal of the Immaculate Conception. But so many miracles occurred in connection with it that the people began to call it the Miraculous Medal.

For 46 years, Catherine told no one of her apparitions except her confessor, Fr. Jean Marie Aladel, as Mary had instructed her. Shortly after receiving the Habit of the Order, Catherine left the motherhouse and took up her duties in the hospice for old men at Enghien. There, in humble uninterrupted service, she passed her life, her hands at work and her heart with God, and her lips closed on her secret.

On December 31, 1876, having received the last sacraments, she died. A sister said, "I've never seen a death so sweet and so calm."

Fifty-six years later, on March 31, 1933, her body was exhumed for the beatification process. It was found incorrupt; the flesh was intact, the limbs supple, and the pupils of her eyes blue.

Today she rests in the motherhouse chapel at Rue du Bac under the altar of the Blessed Virgin of the Globe where Mary had appeared to her a century before.

On July 27, 1947, Pope Pius XII canonized her and called her "The Saint of Silence."

Our Lady wishes this medal to be worn around the neck, and she has promised to grant abundant graces to all who wear it with confidence. It will still work miracles for those who believe.

*   *   *

The Saint Benedict Medal.

St. Benedict was the father of Western Monasticism. His "Rule for Monks" was epoch making and a sure guide to sanctity in any age. Beginning in 520, he founded twelve monasteries in the neighborhood of Subiaco. The foundation at Monte Cassino (529) became the cradle of his Order.

Benedict had great love for the liturgy. Even to this day, the Benedictine Order is noted for its devotion to the liturgy. Benedict always taught, "Prefer nothing to the work of God" (Opus Dei). His twin sister was St. Scholastica. Benedict died March 21 around 542.

Benedict often used the Sign of the Cross to ward off demons and protect himself from being poisoned.

His medal has exceptional power against the demons of Hell and against physical evils. It also has great power in obtaining exceptional graces.

FRONT   BACK

The front of the medal shows St. Benedict holding a cross in one hand and the book of his Rule in the other. Flanking him on each side are the words: *Crux S. Patris Benedicti* (The Cross of the Holy Father Benedict). Below his feet are these words: *Ex S M Casino* MDCCCLXXX (From the Holy Mount of Cassino, 1880). On that date, Monte Cassino was given the exclusive right to produce this medal. Inscribed in the circle surrounding Benedict are the words: *Ejus in obitu nostro presentia muniamur* (May his presence protect us in the hour of death).

The other side of the medal is where the real exorcistic force reveals itself. In the center is the Cross. Benedict loved the Cross and often used it to drive away demons.

The vertical beam of the Cross has five letters: C.S.S.M.L., meaning *Crux Sacra Sit Mihi Lux* (May the holy Cross be for me a light).

The horizontal beam of the Cross also has five letters: N.D.S.M.D., meaning *Non Draco Sit Mihi Dux* (May the dragon never be my guide).

The four large letters at the angles of the Cross: C S P B stand for *Crux Sancti Patris Benedicti* (The Cross of the Holy Father Benedict).

Encircling the Cross in a circle around the right margin are these letters: V.R.S.N.S.M.V., meaning *Vade retro Satana; nunquam suade mihi vana* (Get behind me, Satan; never suggest vain thoughts to me).

Around the left margin of the circle are these letters: S.M.Q.L.I.V.B., meaning *Sunt mala quae libas; ipse venena bibas* (The drinks you offer are evils; drink the poison yourself).

At the top of the circle is the word: *PAX* (Peace).

This highly indulgenced medal can be worn around the neck or attacked to one's Rosary or simply carried in one's pocket. One's personal devotion, together with the powerful blessing and prayers of the Church, make it a formidable weapon against the evil spirits and a mighty help in keeping pure, in bringing about conversions and in guarding against contagious diseases.

*　　*　　*

Captain Myles Walter Keogh.

Every year in Auburn, New York, there is "The Great Race," but the real name of the nation's largest triathlon is "The Capt. Myles Keogh Paddle, Wheel and Run."

Myles Keogh was born March 25, 1840, in County Carlow, Ireland. He received good Catholic training in a local Jesuit school. In 1860 he left Ireland to join the Papal army of Pope Pius IX in conflict with Garibaldi's revolutionaries. For gallantry and heroic bravery, Keogh was decorated with the much coveted "Medaglia di Pro Petri Sede" (the Medals of the Chair of Peter), and he always wore them around his neck with his Scapular.

In 1860, William Seward, President Lincoln's Secretary of State, was searching for military talent, since the federal army was weakened by the defection to the Confederacy of many of the leaders of the nation's standing army. Seward had sent Abp. John Hughes of New York to England and France to keep them from intervening on the side of the South. The Archbishop also visited the Vatican. While in Rome, he recruited three young Irish Papal guards for the Northern army: Daniel Keily, Joseph O'Keefe and Myles Keogh.

Keogh participated in over 100 Civil War battles. After the war, he met Andrew Alexander who was married to Evy Martin of Auburn. This

Auburn, especially with Nelly who was Keogh's age. For the next ten years, Myles was a periodic visitor to the Martin home.

Everyone was delighted when the young Irishman in 1866 received a commission as Captain in the newly-formed 7th U.S. Cavalry under the command of General George Armstrong Custer.

In 1876 the government ordered the Cavalry to round up Indians who had strayed from their reservations to hunt buffalo and to force them to return. There had been abusive practices by many government agents, and the warriors were in a hostile mood.

When the 7th Cavalry left Fort Abraham Lincoln, Dakota Territory, on May 17, Capt. Keogh had a foreboding about his fate. In his last letter to Nelly Martin, he wrote, "We leave Monday on an Indian expedition, and if I ever return, I will go on and see you all. I have requested to be packed up and shipped to Auburn in case I am killed, and I desire to be buried there. God bless you all. Remember if I should die—you may believe that I loved you and every member of your family; it was a second home to me."

Keogh was killed in the Battle of the Little Big Horn, June 25, 1876—Custer's Last Stand. When the fighting was over, the victorious warriors gathered around "the bravest man the Sioux ever fought." As they were stripping his body, they came upon his Scapular and the papal medals in a leather case attached to a cord around his neck. The warriors knew that this was powerful medicine, and so they refused to take chances with it. Therefore, none of the warriors, squaws or old men and boys would desecrate the body. Instead, the propped it up against a tree and left it unmutilated—the only body so left.

On October 25, 1877, a dignified military service was held in Fort Hill Cemetery, Auburn, N.Y., at the Martin family plot. Nelly, who dearly loved Keogh, chose the tombstone and inscribed on it the beautiful lines from Bayard Taylor's "Song of the Camp":

Sleep soldier! Still in honored rest
Your truth and valor wearing.
The bravest are the tenderest,
The loving are the daring.

John Wayne mentions Capt. Myles Keogh in the film, "She Wore a Yellow Ribbon."

Chapter 7

THE ROSARY

Our Lady in speaking of the sacramentals to Mariamante said that *"the Scapular and the Rosary are the greatest of these and will afford you the most protection"* (*The Apostolate of Holy Motherhood*, p. 10).

To Father Stefano Gobbi, Our Lady said:

"The prayer of my predilection is the holy Rosary.

*"For this reason, in my many apparitions I always ask that it be recited. **I unite myself with those who say it;** I request it from all with solicitude and maternal preoccupation"* (*To the Priests, Her Beloved Sons*, #275).

Note that Our Lady says that she unites herself with those who say it. We say, "pray for us now. . ."; and Mary says she does; and her prayers are all-powerful. That is why the Rosary is a powerhouse of graces.

Again, Our Lady said to Fr. Gobbi on the feast of the Holy Rosary (Oct. 7, 1979):

*"By this prayer, you offer your Heavenly Mother a powerful force in intervening for the salvation of many of my poor straying children...Your entire Rosary is like an immense chain of love and salvation with which you are able to encircle persons and situations, and **even to influence all the events of your time**...The Rosary is the prayer which I myself came down from Heaven to ask of you.*

"By it you are able to lay bare the plots of my adversary; you escape from many of his deceits; you defend yourselves from many dangers which he puts in your way; it preserves you from evil and brings you even closer to me, because I am able to be truly your guide and protection."

Fr. Gobbi told us priests once that, when he was in Yugoslavia giving a cenacle to the priests in Zagreb and was walking in a woods, a huge dog came out of nowhere, snarling savagely at him and seeming ready to pounce on him. Father said he was terrified. He didn't know what to do. All he had in his hand was the Rosary which he had been praying. When the savage dog came toward him, he instinctively hit him with his Rosary. When he did, the dog stopped and grew smaller. He hit it again and again; and each time, the dog whined and grew smaller and smaller until it was smaller than a pup. Then he kicked it away. Father said that the dog was the devil, and he was powerless against the Rosary.

So Mary begs us to give her the garlands of our Rosaries, recited often and with great devotion. For, she says, *"It is the weapon which is to be used by you today in fighting and winning this bloody battle; it is the golden chain that binds you to my heart; it is the lightning rod that will keep far from you, and from those who are dear to you, the fire of the chastisement; it is the sure means of having me always close to you"* (Idem, #264).

Father Gobbi said that one day he complained to the Blessed Virgin Mary. "Mother," he said to her, "I am sick and tired of having mothers come to me and telling me that they raised their sons or daughters up in the faith, but that now they have left the Church and are going deeper and deeper into sin. What shall I tell them?"

You know what Mary promised Fr. Gobbi? She said, *"Tell these parents if they say the Rosary daily for their children, I will take care of them."* What a wonderful promise that is! It is such a consolation to so many parents today who are having the same experience with their own children. Mary says, "Don't worry. Just say my Rosary for them, and I'll take care of them." And she will if—if you pray the Rosary daily for them. Trust her.

Let me conclude these few thoughts on the Rosary with the words of a great saint, St. Louis de Montfort. He wrote: "If you say the Rosary faithfully until death, I do assure you that, in spite of the gravity of your sins, you will receive a never fading crown of glory. Even if you are on the brink of damnation, even if you have one foot in Hell...sooner or later you will be converted and will amend your life and save your soul, IF—and mark well what I say—IF you say the Rosary devoutly every day until death" (*The Secret of the Rosary*, p. 10).

If you desire to get a fuller treatment of the power of the Rosary, read my booklet titled *The Power of the Rosary*.

*   *   *

What does the Church think about the Rosary?

This is one of the five devotions to which she attaches a plenary indulgence. And note, she attaches the same indulgence to the family recitaton of the Rosary. Here is what she says:

Recitation of the Marian Rosary
(Rosarii marialis recitatio)

A *plenary indulgence* is granted, if the Rosary is recited in a church or public oratory or in a family group, a religious Community or pious Association; a *partial indulgence* is granted in other circumstances.

Now the Rosary is a certain formula of prayer, which is made up of fifteen decades of 'Hail Marys' with an 'Our Father' before each decade, and in which the recitation of each decade is accompanied by pious meditation on a particular mystery of our Redemption." *(Roman Breviary)*

The name "Rosary," however, is commonly used in reference to only a third part of the fifteen decades.

The gaining of the plenary indulgence is regulated by the following norms:

1) The recitation of a third part only of the Rosary suffices; but the five decades must be recited continuously.

2) The *vocal* recitation must be accompanied by pious meditation on the mysteries.

3) In public recitation the mysteries must be announced in the manner customary in the place; for private recitation, however, it suffices if the *vocal* recitation is accompanied by meditation on the mysteries.

(Enchirdion, #48)

Chapter 8

THE WAY OF THE CROSS

The Way of the Cross is simply a series of pictures representing scenes in the passion of Our Lord. Technically, the Stations of the Cross do not consist in these artistic representations but in the wooden crosses located above the designs.

In Our Lord's Passion, He carried a cross from the court of Pontius Pilate to the hill of Calvary. Hence the name "Way of the Cross."

On the way, Christ was obliged to stop awhile and rest. Tht is why the Way of the Cross is sometimes called the "Stations of the Cross," for station means a stopping-place. A station is where a train stops, a depot. An English pilgrim, William Wey, in the late 1400s was the first to call the customary stopping places of Our Lord on the *Via Dolorosa* "stations." Incidentally, at that time, the stations started on Calvary and went back to Pilate's court. It was in the next century that the Way of the Cross was reversed to the order that we follow today.

From Pilate to the tomb, Christ stopped fourteen times, twelve times while alive and two while dead. Because of the fact that, of the fourteen stations as we now have them, only seven are mentioned in the gospel, and two others (the stripping and nailing to the cross) are implied in the gospels, and because Christianity does not end in the tomb, Pope Paul VI in 1975 approved a whole new set of stations, beginning with the Last Supper and ending with the Resurrection—all based on the Scriptures. As far as I know, this new version has not yet replaced the old Way of the Cross, which is rooted deeply in the hearts and minds of the faithful and adorn the walls of almost every Catholic church.

Origin. To whom do we owe this holy exercise? Much of the Way of the Cross is based on Tradition. It is very likely that the Way of the Cross owes its origin to the Mother of God. In the Revelations of St. Bridget, Our Lady said:

> *"For all the time that I lived after the Ascension of my Son, I visited the places in which He suffered and showed His wonders. So rooted, too, was His Passion in my heart, that whether I ate or worked, it was ever as if fresh in memory"* (p. 67).

Again Our Lady told St. Bridget:

> *"Some years after the Ascension of my Son, I was one day much afflicted with*

a longing to rejoin my Son. Then I beheld
a radiant angel, such as I had before seen,
who said to me, 'Thy Son, who is Our Lord
and God, sent me to announce to thee that
the time is at hand when thou shalt come
bodily to Him, to receive the crown pre-
pared for thee.'"

She went on to tell St. Bridget that the angel
disappeared and that she prepared herself for
her departure by *"going, as was my wont, to all*
the spots where my Son had suffered; and when
one day my mind was absorbed in admiring con-
templation of divine charity, my soul was filled
therein with such exultation that it could not con-
tain itself, and in that very consideration, my soul
was loosed from the body."

Two beautiful thoughts, I think, are here. First,
Mary died from love. As harp strings burst asun-
der with the music they throb to express, so Mary
died of love. And secondly, she died while making the Stations of the Cross. And I like to believe
that it was while contemplating the great love
of Jesus shown on the cross of Calvary that her
heart burst from love. In other words, I like to
think that she died on Calvary just like her Son.

What happened was that the early Christians
began to follow Mary's example. At first, some
of the Christian women went with her to the
way of Our Lord's cross. After her death, the
Way of the Cross became the first place for Chris-

tian pilgrims to visit and to make. This gave rise to processions—always preceded with a cross at the head. Even today a cross-bearer leads our processions.

If you go to Jerusalem, one of the musts is to make the Via Dolorosa:

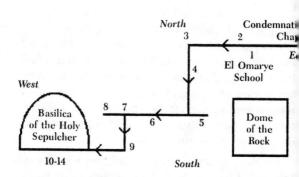

When the Church was persecuted by Rome, the pagan emperors tried to stop these processions along the way of the cross by erecting statues of their gods and goddesses at these sacred spots. They reasoned that Christians would not go near the shrines of pagan gods. Unwittingly, however, they thus preserved the spots of Our Lord's Passion.

In 324, St. Helena went to the Holy Land to find the true cross of Christ in thanksgiving for the victory of her son, Constantine the Great, over Maxentius at the Milvian Bridge (312 A.D.)—a victory won because of the cross as we read in Chapter 3. Before this decisive battle, Constantine had a vision of a cross in the sky with the words: *In Hoc Signo Vinces*) ("In this sign thou shalt conquer"). Constantine put the cross atop his battle standards. The rest is history. He conquered Maxentius and became sole ruler of the Roman Empire.

So St. Helena, his mother, went to Jerusalem in quest of the true cross. The pagan shrines told her right where to look. When she found the true cross, she erected a great basilica, called Holy Sepulchre, because it is built over both the tomb of Christ and the hill of Calvary. Thus, in the basilica are the last four Stations of the cross.

When the Mohammedans captured Jerusalem in the seventh century, they forbade Christians to go to the holy places. So representations of Our Lord's Way of the Cross were put on the walls of churches. When Christians could no longer go to Jerusalem, Jerusalem came to the Christians.

* * *

What does the Church think about the Way of the Cross?

The Church so highly prizes this devotion that she has richly indulgenced it. In her revision of indulgences, the Church has retained only five

plenary indulgences—only five. One of these is
for making the Way of the Cross.

Here are the norms the Church has set for
gaining the indulgence.

Exercise of the Way of the Cross
(Viae Crucis exercitium)

A *plenary indulgence* is granted to the faithful,
who make the pious exercise of the *Way of the
Cross.*

In the pious exercise of the *Way of the Cross*
we recall anew the sufferings, which the divine
Redeemer endured, while going from the praeto-
rium of Pilate, where he was condemned to death,
to the mount of Calvary, where he died on the
cross for our salvation.

The gaining of the plenary indulgence is regulated by the following norms:

1) The pious exercise must be made before
sttions of the *Way of the Cross* legitimately
erected.

2) For the erection of the *Way of the Cross*
fourteen crosses are required, to which it is customary to add fourteen pictures or images, which
represent the stations of Jerusalem.

3) According to the more common practice,
the pious exercise consists of fourteen pious readings, to which some vocal prayers are added. *However, nothing more is required than a pious
meditation on the Passion and Death of the Lord,
which need not be a particular consideration of
the individual mysteries of the stations.*

4) A *movement* from one station to the next is required.

But if the pious exercise is made publicly and if it is not possible for all taking part to go in an orderly way from station to station, it suffices if at least the *one conducting the exercise goes from station to station, the others remaining in their place.*

Those who are "impeded" can gain the same indulgence, if they spend at least one half an hour in pious reading and meditation on the Passion and Death of Our Lord Jesus Christ.

(*Enchiridion,* #63)

Chapter 9

READING OF SACRED SCRIPTURES

Vatican II, in its document on Divine Revelation wrote: "The Church has always venerated the divine Scriptures just as she venerates the body of the Lord" (#21).

That's a startling statement. The Church is saying she puts the word of God on a par with the Holy Eucharist. Thus, in her restructing of the Mass, she has built it on the twin pylons of the Liturgy of the Word and the Liturgy of the Eucharist.

When Israel fell upon hard times after their return from the Babylonian Captivity, the scribe Ezra revived their sinking spirits by reading to the people the Word of God (*Nehemiah* 8:2-10). To make sure they would always be uplifted, Ezra founded the synagogue service which consists of two readings, one from the Law and one from the Prophets.

And when Jesus came "to announce a year of favor from the Lord," He began His public life in a synagogue by reading from the Scriptures, the prophet Isaiah (*Luke* 4:14-21).

Today Satan has targeted two objects, families and the priesthood. He is breaking up marriages by creating dissension between husbands and wives, between parents and children and children and parents. We have two weapons to conquer this onslaught by the powers of darkness; one is the family Rosary, and the other is famly Bible reading.

Here is what the Mother of God said in her messages at Medjugorje.

To Jelena, April 19, 1984, Mary said:

> *"I'm going to reveal a spiritual secret to you: if you want to be stronger than evil, make yourself a plan of personal prayer. Take a certin time in the morning, read a text from Holy Scripture, anchor the Divine Word in your heart, and strive to live it during the day, particularly during the moment of trials. In this way, you will be stronger than evil.*

On Thursday, October 18, 1984, she said to the visionaries:

> *"Dear children! Today I ask you to read the Bible in your homes every day. Place it in a visible place there, where it will always remind you to read it and to pray."*

On Thursday, February 14, 1985, Our Lady said to Maria:

> *"Every family must pray and read the Bible."*

The Bible is a unique book. It is God's book. He inspired it. He is its author. Thus, we call it the "Word of God." So holy is it, that after reading the gospel, the priest kisses the Word of God.

Therefore, the Bible must not be treated like every other book. Our Lady said to place it in a visible place, not on an out-of-the-way book-shelf with other books. It is God's book. It deserves preferential treatment. The Bible should be enthroned in your homes.

Get a table. Put it in a conspicuous place. Put a white cloth on it, then a crucifix. In St. Paul's Cathedral in London, under the crucifix are written the words, "This is how God loved the world."

On each side of the crucifix place a picture of the Sacred Heart and one of the Immaculate Heart of Mary. The sin of the angels was pride; the sin of people is forgetfulness. Out of sight, out of mind. We need reminders, images.

Then place the Bible on the table, but opened. Blessings will pour out on the home, just as a fragrant aroma will fill the room when a bottle of perfume is opened or incense is burned.

Then place a rosary there, which is simply walking through the life of Christ with Mary.

Finally, put a bottle of Holy Water on the table—a powerful bug repellent, the bugs being the demons of Hell—a screen to keep out the infernal pests.

So, besides the sacramentals you wear, your home altar will have all the others.

Let's get back to reading the Bible. Assign a member of the family to be responsible for turning over a page each day, and perhaps to pick out a passage to discuss at the supper table. The members of the family can take turns at this each week.

Then get in the habit of giving the Bible as a gift—at weddings, at graduation; and for children, a picture Bible.

Remember the Bible is God's Word, and the words of God are spirit and life (*Jn.* 6:64).

* * *

What does the Church think of reading the Bible?

Here is what the Church says: "A *partial indulgence* is granted to the faithful, who with the venertion due the Divine Word, make a spiritual reading from Sacred Scripture. A *plenary indulgence* is granted, if this reading is continued for at least one half an hour" (*Enchiridion*, #50).

Appendix

BLESSING OF HOLY WATER

1. On Sundays and whenever it is necessary, the salt and clean water to be blessed are prepared in the church or in the sacristy. The priest vests in surplice and violet stole and begins:

V. Our help is in the name of the Lord.

R. Who made Heaven and earth.

2. Then he begins the exorcism of the salt.

O salt, creature of God, I exorcise you by the living † God, by the † true God, by the holy † God, by the God who ordered you to be poured into the water by Eliseus the prophet so that its life-giving powers might be restored.

I exorcise you so that you may become a means of salvation for believers, that you may bring health of soul and body to all who make use of you, and *that you may put to flight and drive away* from the places where you are sprinkled every apparition, villainy, and turn of devilish deceit, and every unclean spirit, adjured by him who will come to judge the living and the dead and the world by fire. R. Amen.

Let us pray.

Almighty and everlasting God, we humbly implore you, in your immeasurable kindness and love, to bless † this salt which you created and gave to the use of mankind, so that it may become a source of health for the minds and bodies of all who make use of it. May it rid whatever it touches or sprinkles of all uncleanness and protect it from every assault of evil spirits. Through Our Lord, Jesus Christ, your Son, who lives and reigns with you in the unity of the Holy Spirit, God, forever and ever. R. Amen.

EXORCISM OF THE WATER

He continues:

O water, creature of God, I exorcise you in the name of God the Father † almighty, and in the name of Jesus † Christ his Son, Our Lord, and in the power of the Holy † Spirit. *I exorcise you* so that you may put to flight all the *power* of the enemy, and be able to root out and supplant that enemy with his apostate angels: through the power of Our Lord Jesus Christ, who will come to judge the living and the dead and the world by fire. R. Amen.

Let us pray.

O God, for the salvation of mankind you built your greatest mysteries on this substance, water, in your kindness hear our prayers and pour down the power of your blessing † into this element made ready for many kinds of purifications. May this, your creature, become an agent of divine grace in the service of your mysteries, *to drive away evil spirits* and dispel sickness, so that everything in the homes and other buildings of the faithful that is sprinkled with this water may be rid of all uncleanness and freed from every harm. Let no breath of infection, no disease-bearing air remain in these places. May the wiles of the lurking enemy prove of no avail. Let whatever might menace the safety and peace of those who live here be put to flight by the sprinkling of this water, so that the health obtained by calling upon your holy name may be made secure against all attack. Through Christ Our Lord. *R*. Amen.

3. Here he pours salt into the water in the form of a cross, saying:

May a mixture of salt and water now be made, in the name of the Father, and of the † Son, and of the Holy Spirit. *R*. Amen.

V. The Lord be with you.

R. And with your spirit.

Let us pray.

O God, Creator unconquerable, invincible King, Victor ever-glorious, you hold in check the forces bent on dominating us, you overcome the cruelty of the raging enemy, in your power you beat down the wicked foe.

Humbly and fearfully do we pray to you, O Lord, and we ask you to look with favor on this salt and water which you created. Shine on it with the light of your kindness. Sanctify it by the dew of your love, so that, through the invocation of your holy name, wherever this water and salt is sprinkled it may turn aside every attack of the unclean spirit and dispel the terror of the poisonous serpent. And wherever we may be, make the Holy Spirit present to us who now implore your mercy. Through Christ Our Lord. R. Amen.

SCAPULAR RITUAL FOR PRIESTS

PRIEST: Show us, O Lord, Thy mercy.
ALL: And grant us Thy salvation.
PRIEST: O Lord, hear my prayer.
ALL: And let my cry come unto Thee.
PRIEST: The Lord be with you.
ALL: And with your spirit.
PRIEST: Let us pray.

O Lord Jesus Christ, Savior of mankind, * by Thy right hand sanctify † these Scapulars (this Scapular) * which Thy servants will devoutly wear for the love of Thee * and of Thy Mother, the Blessed Virgin Mary of Mt. Carmel; * so that, by her intercession, * they may be protected from the wickedness of the enemy and persevere in Thy grace until death; * Who lives and reignest for ever and ever.

The priest now sprinkles the Scapular with Holy Water, after which he places the Scapular on each one saying:

PRIEST: Receive this blessed Scapular and ask the Most Holy Virgin that, by her merits, it may be worn with no stain of sin and may protect you from all harm and bring you into everlasting life.

ALL: Amen.

PRIEST: By the power granted to me, I admit you to a share in all the spiritual works performed; with the merciful help of Jesus Christ, by the Religious of Mount Carmel; in the name of the Father, and of the Son † and of the Holy Spirit.

ALL: Amen.

PRIEST: May Almighty God.

Creator of Heaven and earth, bless † you * whom He has been pleased to receive into the Confraternity of the Blessed Virgin Mary of Mount Carmel. * We beg her to crush the head of the ancient serpent in the hour of your death, * and, in the end, to obtain for you a palm and the crown of your everlasting inheritance. * Through Christ Our Lord. Amen.

The priest now sprinkles those enrolled with Holy Water.